Contents

The Glen, on the beach at Babbacombe, Devon.

The Man They Could Not
HANG

John Bilyard

Published in association with
The Basic Skills Agency

Hodder & Stoughton

A MEMBER OF THE HODDER HEADLINE GROUP

Acknowledgements
Cover: Matthew Williams
Photo: p. iv © Terry Leaman
Illustrations: Kay Dixey

Every effort has been made to trace copyright holders of material reproduced
in this book. Any rights not acknowledged will be acknowledged in
subsequent printings if notice is given to the publisher.

This story was adapted by the author using newspaper articles taken from
Lloyd's Weekly News, which appeared in the publication in 1908.

Orders: please contact Bookpoint Ltd, 130 Milton Park, Abingdon, Oxon OX14
4SB. Telephone: (44) 01235 827720, Fax: (44) 01235 400454. Lines are open from
9.00 - 6.00, Monday to Saturday, with a 24 hour message answering service.
Email address: orders@bookpoint.co.uk

British Library Cataloguing in Publication Data
A catalogue record for this book is available from The British Library

ISBN 0 340 84846 4

First published 2002
Impression number   10 9 8 7 6 5 4 3 2 1
Year   2006 2005 2004 2003 2002

Typeset by SX Composing DTP, Rayleigh, Essex.
Printed in Great Britain for Hodder & Stoughton Educational, a division of
Hodder Headline Plc, 338 Euston Road, London NW1 3BH by Athenaeum
Press, Gateshead, Tyne & Wear.

1

Babbacombe Lee

My name is Lee.
John Lee.
They call me Babbacombe Lee.

Babbacombe is a little village in Devon.
I went to work there when I was 15.
Babbacombe is a beautiful place.
It sits by the sea.
It is full of fishing boats.
People come there for their holidays.
They go home with wonderful memories.

But my memory of Babbacombe
is quite different.
It is like a nightmare.
The memory just will not go away.
It's the place where my life fell apart.

Many years have passed since then.
Many painful years.
Now I have decided to tell my story.
You may find my story hard to believe.
Many people have called me a liar.
But trust me.
Every word is true.
Truth can be stranger than fiction.

2

Miss Keyse

I was born just a few miles
from Babbacombe.
I loved living in the country.
I had lots of friends.
I sometimes got into trouble.
But that is normal for all children.

When I was 15 my father told me
I had to get a job.
I suppose I was lucky.
I found a job straightaway.
My employer was called Miss Keyse.
She lived in an old house called 'The Glen'.
It was very near the beach at Babbacombe.

Miss Keyse was a lovely lady.
I shall always remember her kind smile.
We got on well from my first day.
I did odd jobs in the house
and looked after Miss Keyse's old horse.
She paid me three shillings a week.
Three shillings is 15p.
But I quickly got bored.

I had plenty of free time.
I used to go down to the beach.
I loved looking at the ships
in Babbacombe Bay.
I loved talking to the old sailors.
They always had exciting stories to tell.
I soon fell in love with the sea.

One day I told my father I wanted to join
the Royal Navy.
He shouted. Mother cried.
But in the end they let me go.

3

Life at Sea

The Navy was great.
I enjoyed travelling.
I loved the smell and roar of the sea.
It was all very exciting.
But we never know what is
round the corner.

One morning I just could not get up.
I ached all over.
The doctor sent me to the hospital.
They say I nearly died of pneumonia.
But the doctors pulled me through.
Then the bad news came.
The doctors said I had to leave the Navy.

I was too weak to do the hard work.
I still have my leaving papers.
My final grade was 'very good.'
It brings tears to my eyes when I read it.

If only I could have stayed in the Navy.
Things would have been so different.
The nightmare may never have happened.

4
The Letter

The only job I could get was in a hotel.
I was the boot boy.
I had to clean the guests' boots and shoes.
My heart ached.

Then a letter arrived.
I knew the neat handwriting
on the envelope.
It was from my old employer, Miss Keyse.
I read her letter slowly.

Dear John,

   I was so sorry to hear your news.
How are you feeling now?
I still need some help at the Glen.
How would you feel about coming back?
Come and see me soon.
We can talk about it.
      Yours sincerely,
      Miss Keyse.

I went to Babbacombe straight away.
Miss Keyse had not changed at all.
She still had that kind smile.
She held out her hand.
Then she kissed me on the cheek.

We soon agreed that I would come back.
I would do general duties in the house.
I would chop wood for the fires
and help the other servants.
I began to feel happy again.

5

Back to The Glen

_____

I soon settled in at The Glen again.
Miss Keyse was a lovely lady to work for.
But then something happened.

Pay day was Thursday.
Miss Keyse called us into her study
one by one.
When it was my turn Miss Keyse smiled.
She handed me two shillings.
'I think you've made a mistake, Miss,'
I said timidly.
My pay is three shillings.'

Miss Keyse blushed.

'I'm sorry, John,' she said.
'Times are hard.
I've had to cut your wages.'

My face went red with anger.
I snatched the two coins from her hand.
I stormed out and slammed the door.
I talked to the other servants.
Miss Keyse had not cut their wages.

6

Fire, fire

It was daybreak on 14 November 1884.
I was awoken by a shout:
'Fire, fire! Somebody help!'
I quickly pulled on my clothes.
All the servants were running around.
The house was full of thick smoke.
I tried to open the window.
In the end I just smashed it with my fist.
We had to have air.
My arm was dripping blood.
A piece of my flesh hung on the glass.
Flames were leaping through the
dining room door.
I put my hand over my mouth and ran in.

Miss Keyse lay on the floor.
Her hands were blue.
They looked like a bird's claws.
Her hair had fallen round her face.
Her eyes stared with the horror of death.
Around her mouth there was
no sign of her kind smile.
Her lips were twisted and her mouth open.
She must have screamed horribly
before she died.

7

Under Arrest

We needed more help to put out the fire.
So I ran into the village.
When I got back several people were there.
There was a policeman at the door.

Someone had lifted Miss Keyse
on to the sofa.
I helped to carry her body outside.
I noticed there was blood on her throat.
The fire was still burning.
Someone shouted,
'We need to chop this beam down.'
I ran to the woodshed and fetched an axe.
I then realised how much my arm hurt.

I had lost a lot of blood.
I got my arm bandaged by the village doctor.
An hour later I was back at The Glen.
The fire was almost out.
I went and sat in the kitchen.

My eyes were still watering from the smoke.
I think I must have been crying too.
Through my misty eyes I saw
three policemen.
The Inspector spoke.
'John Lee, I am arresting you for
the murder of Miss Keyse.
Come along quietly.'

I was too shocked to say a word.
As they led me away,
one of the servants ran up.
'I know you didn't do it, John.
You loved Miss Keyse like a sister.
We all know that.'

8

The Trial Begins

In prison, I waited for my trial to begin.
All I can remember is questions.
The same questions over and over again.
The police had made up their minds.
They said I killed Miss Keyse with the axe.
I was angry because she cut my wages.
I lost my temper.
I killed her with the axe.
Then I set fire to the house
to destroy the evidence.

I always gave the police the same answer.
'I am innocent.'
But they would not listen.

At last, the day of my trial arrived.
Two prison officers marched me up
from my cell.
The court was full of people.
The judge and lawyers wore their
wigs and gowns.
The jury was made up of twelve men.
They looked like statues.
Newspaper reporters sat in their
special seats.
They fiddled with their
pencils and notebooks.
Behind them sat an artist.
He was making sketches.

I looked at the public gallery.
I knew my friends were there.
But I was very confused.
Very confused and very frightened.
I could not make out who they were.
All I could see was eyes staring at me.

I wanted to hide.
But I was the centre of attention.

The clerk read the charge.
'How do you plead?' he asked.
'Not guilty,' I replied in a clear voice.

I listened to the evidence against me.
It was all nonsense.
The lawyer told the court about the axe.
I had fetched it very quickly;
too quickly for it to be in the woodshed.
It must have been in the house.
I had left it there after killing Miss Keyse.

I kept wanting to shout out,
'This is nonsense.
I loved Miss Keyse.'
But what was the point?
In my head I knew what would happen.
Why not get it over with?

9

The Judgement

The trial lasted three days.
Then the judge summed up.
The jury left the court.
They would decide if I was
guilty or innocent.
Whether I would live or die.
They took me down to my cell.

At last my cell door opened again.
It was nearly all over.

The prison officers marched me
up to the dock.
The judge and jury came back in.

Every eye was on me.
The foreman of the jury stood up.
'Do you find the accused guilty
or not guilty?' boomed the judge.

There seemed to be a long, long silence.
'Guilty.'
Two more prison officers
now stood behind me.
They held my arms tightly.
The judge put a black cap over his wig.
I only remember parts of what he said.
But these words stick in my mind:

'You will be hanged by the neck
until you are dead.
Take him down.'

I gripped the edge of the dock.
'God knows I'm innocent,' I screamed.
They took me back to prison.

10

Condemned

I was now in Exeter Prison.
I would stay here until they hanged me.

I had to wear prison clothes.
Two prison officers were with me.
They watched me day and night.
They cut my food up for me.
I was not allowed to have a knife.
I could not have a razor either.
I quickly grew a scruffy beard.

Mother and father came to see me.
My father broke down when he saw me.
My mother was very brave.

One day the Governor came to see me.
The date of my execution was fixed.
The hangman would do his work
on 23 February, 1885.
He didn't understand why I smiled.
'Why are you smiling, Lee?'
'Because I'm innocent, Sir,' I replied.
He said nothing after that.

11

The Trap Door

The night before my execution,
I was tormented by bad dreams
the whole night.
They woke me early the next day.
The Chaplain came to see me.
He was very kind and spoke gently to me.
'This is your last chance to confess, John.
Clear your conscience before you die.'

I could say only three words:
'I am innocent.'
Then I heard the prison bell.
Long, deep, slow notes.
Each one was like a weight on my chest.

At five to eight my cell door opened.
The Governor came in.
The hangman was behind him.
He reached out to shake my hand.
That struck me as strange.
I put my hand out.
It all happened quickly.
He put a thick leather belt round my waist.
He strapped my arms behind my back.
My stomach turned to ice.

We walked slowly through the prison.
The bell was still tolling.
It was like a funeral procession.

We came outside.
Ahead of me was a huge shed.
The doors were flung open.
A rope dangled from the beams.
Three prison officers stood by the door.

They stood me on a wooden trap door.
I heard it creak as I stood on it.
I stood to attention.
I could hear the birds singing.

The hangman put a hood over my head.
It was like a large pillowcase.
Then I felt the rope round my neck.
It was thicker than I expected.
The hangman pulled the rope tight.
I felt the hard knot under my right ear.
The hangman's fingers smelt of tobacco.

The prison bell stopped.
A voice said, 'Drop away!'
I heard a grating noise under my feet.
It was like a bolt being pulled back.
My heart was bursting in my chest.
I curled my toes up.
I was like a bird trying to hold
on to a branch.

I felt the trap door open.

Then there was a jolt. It had jammed.

I stood there poised between
life and death.

I heard the sound of heavy boots.

They were stamping on the trap door.

But nothing happened.

Over and over again they tried
to make the trap door open.

I felt the sweat run down my face.

In the end they took me out.
I could hear them testing the trap door.
Someone oiled the hinges.
A voice said, 'It's all right now.
Bring him back.'
I was going to meet death
a second time.

I stood on the trap door once more.
I was trembling and sweating.
'Drop!' called a voice.
I heard the bolt draw back.
I felt a jolt.
The trap door had jammed again.
I started falling to the ground.
The warders held me up.

'For God's sake get him off,'
yelled the Governor.
They took me outside.
The cold air brought me round.

I heard angry voices coming
from the shed.
Everyone was blaming everyone else.
They took the hood off my head.
It was a beautiful day.
I could not believe I was still alive.
But I knew it was not for long.

They kept testing the trap door.
It crashed open again and again.
Finally I heard a voice.
'We've got it this time.
Bring him in.'

Again, I was on the trap door.
'Drop!' yelled a voice.
But nothing happened at all.
'Drop, damn it!' cried the voice again.
But my feet stayed firmly
on the trap door.
I woke up in my cell two hours later.

12

Prison Sentence

The Governor came to see me.
'You poor fellow,' he said.
'How you must have suffered.
We have tried to hang you three times.
We cannot try again. That is the law.
You are not meant to die.
I wish we could let you go.
But you have still been found guilty.
You must stay in prison for twenty years.'

And so I grew old in prison.
Now I have found freedom again.
But I shall always be the prisoner
of my memories.